MINDFUL MOMENTS

FOR THE MODERN MAN

This Book Belongs To

_____

Making mindfulness moments in your day
couldn't be easier with this
Mindful Moments for the Modern Man

This purpose-built coloring in book
has been brought to you by the creators at
Paperdoll Publications
and it is our wish that you use this book as a tool to
colour your way beyond the everyday distractions
that this modern world can inflict.
It is our wish that you use this book as a tool to be
mindful, self-loving, and accepting.

No thinking. Just "BE."
This space is solely yours.
There are no rules to use this book, no deadlines, no
expectations, just loving awareness in this safe space.
It's you; the pages... and nothing else.
Breathe, release and... relax.

Paperdoll Publications

Autumn leaves fall
In the silent still of night
Peaceful and serene.

In the stillness calm
Mindful thoughts flow like a stream
Peace found within, now

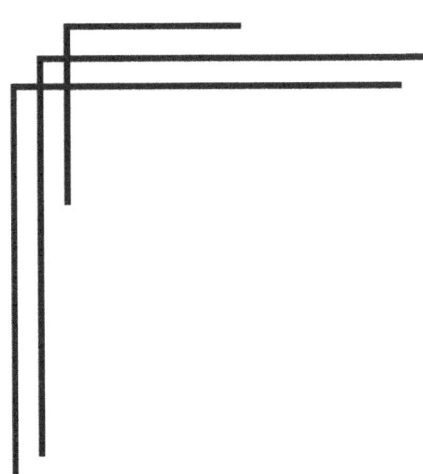

Breathing Exercises

Deep breathing

Inhale slowly through your nose, hold for a few seconds, then exhale slowly through your mouth. Repeat for several breaths.

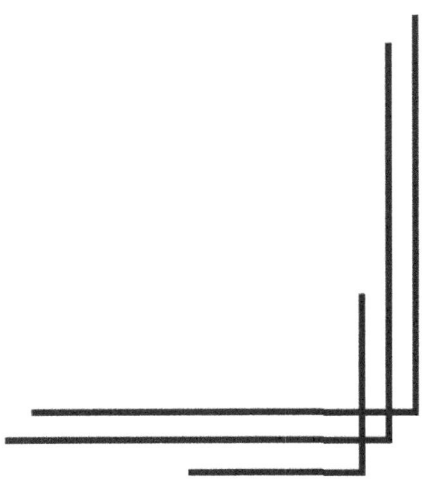

Gently swaying trees
Peaceful rustling leaves, heard
Calmness take me whole

Tall trees reaching high
Nature's symphony surrounds
Peace in the green woods.

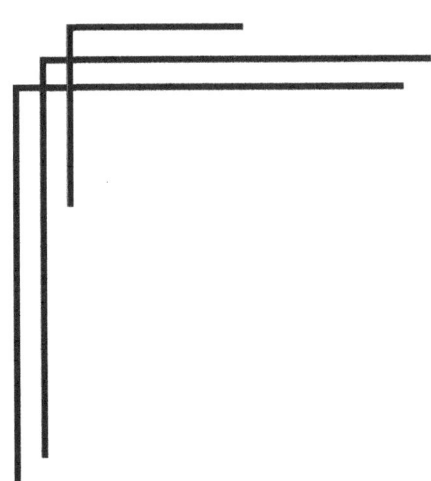

Breathing Exercises

Progressive muscle relaxation

Tense and then relax different
muscle groups in your body,
starting from your feet and working
your way up to your head.

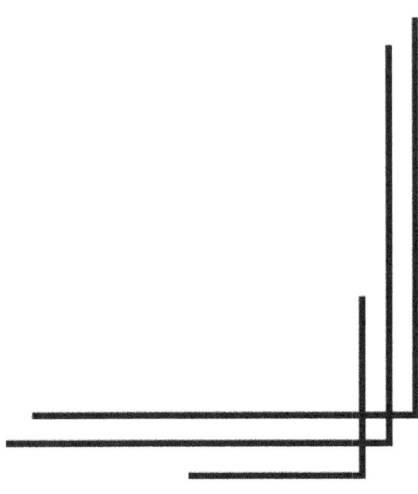

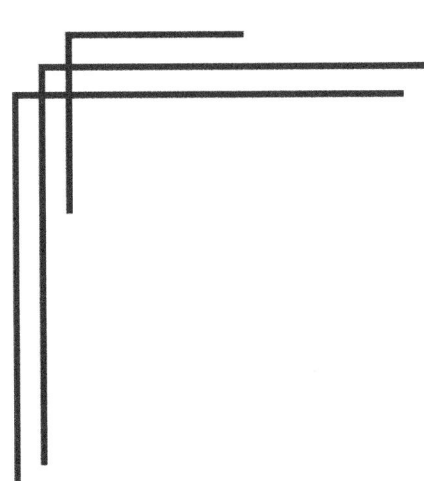

Breathing Exercises

Box breathing

Inhale for 4 counts, hold for 4 counts, exhale for 4 counts, and hold for 4 counts. Repeat for several cycles.

Ocean waves crash
Soothing sound, peaceful and calm
Nature's symphony

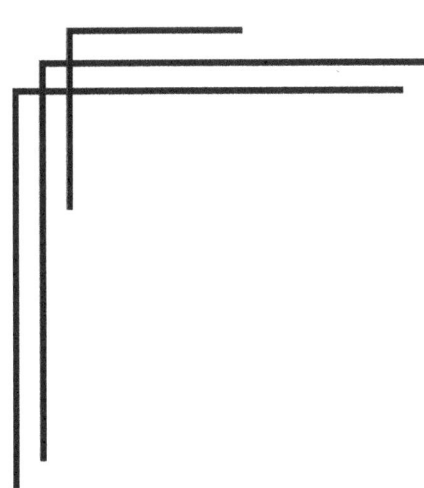

Breathing Exercises

Body scan meditation

Lie down and focus on relaxing each part of your body, starting from your toes and working your way up to your head.

White sand, blue skies
Sun warms skin, wind in my hair
Peaceful beach escape

Waves dance and play near
Shells and seaweed in the sand
Nature's artwork seen

Breeze dances by, cool
Carries scents, whispers in ear
Nature's gentle voice.

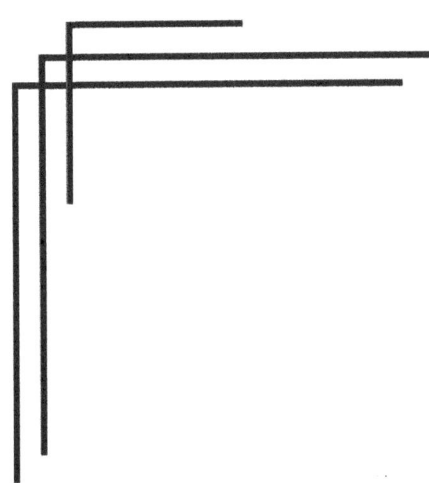

Breathing Exercises

Alternate Nostril Breathing

Close your right nostril and inhale through your left nostril. Then, close your left nostril and exhale through your right nostril. Repeat for several breaths.

Made in the USA
Las Vegas, NV
06 April 2023

70279451R00077